Overcoming Negative Self-Talk with the Truth of the Gospel

by
John Stange

~ *Ivystream Press* ~

Philadelphia, Pennsylvania

JOHN STANGE

JOHN STANGE

Table of Contents

If you enjoy this book, you may also enjoy some of John Stange's other books, including...

Overcoming Anxiety
12 powerful truths from Scripture for defeating worry and fear

Words that Sting
How to handle destructive criticism like Jesus

Building a Christ Centered Marriage
7 Keys for keeping Jesus at the center of your relationship

Everyday Faith (Volume 1)
31 Daily Devotions from the Book of Jude

Too Busy for What Matters Most
6 Priorities of the Christian Life that We Must Make Time for Today

What is Heaven Really Like?
Biblical Answers to the 10 Biggest Questions about Life After Death

Your Identity in Christ
100 Powerful Reminders of Who you Truly are in Jesus

What did Jesus say about Marriage?
What did Christ teach about marriage and how

should I live in response.

Praying what Jesus Prayed for the Church
A devotional look at Christ's prayer in John 17

~

Follow John Stange on Facebook and you'll be notified of his new releases, reduced prices and free book promotions.
https://www.facebook.com/author.john.stange

If you're interested in contacting the author or learning more about his ministry and other books, be sure to visit his website:
JohnStange.com

Getting Started

Every person has a recording that plays over and over in their mind. We repeatedly tell ourselves things that may or may not be true on a daily basis. Some of the things we tell ourselves are accurate, encouraging, edifying and Christ-centered. But just as often, we tell ourselves things that are completely untrue and the fruit of false beliefs or a false gospel that we've allowed to take root in our heart.

Some people spend the bulk of their lives engaging in negative self-talk. They keep themselves in a constant state of discouragement and mental defeat with the words and mantras they repeat to themselves every single day. But Christ wants more for His people. The truth of His Gospel is rich and deep and this truth has the power to counteract the negativity and false beliefs that try to take root in our lives and our thinking.

In this book, we will be examining the only message that can defeat our negative self-talk for good. The Gospel of Jesus Christ is good news for the hurting and discouraged soul. The coming pages and chapters are all geared toward pointing our hearts back to Christ and learning to see ourselves from His loving and gracious perspective.

We'll also take a look at a simple, but effective, 7-step process that we can implement when we're ready to overcome the daily presence of negative self-talk in our lives.

If you've been repeating a stream of negative self-talk to yourself for years, this book is for you. My hope is that after reading through these pages, you'll feel equipped with the truth of Christ's Gospel as well as a helpful technique that can help you identify, address and counteract the pattern of negativity and discouragement you've been struggling with.

Disclaimer: *This book is for information and motivation purposes only. While it's content is helpful, it is not a substitute for the specific counsel of a doctor or mental health professional who is fully acquainted with your specific needs. This book is not intended as a substitute for the medical advice of your physician. The reader should regularly consult a physician in matters relating to his/her health and particularly with respect to any symptoms that may require diagnosis or medical attention.*

--

John Stange has been serving in pastoral ministry

*for nearly 20 years. He is the Lead Pastor of Core Creek Community Church in Langhorne, Pennsylvania. In addition to his pastoral work, John is also an author, speaker and leadership coach. His podcast **"Leadership Laughter"** was recently selected by iTunes for their "New & Noteworthy" distinction.*

*John specializes in writing concise books and devotionals that are "long enough to provoke thought, but short enough that you'll actually finish them." Please visit his author page on Amazon or **JohnStange.com** for more of his recent titles and new releases.*

JOHN STANGE

Chapter 1.
What is Negative Self-Talk?

The phrase "negative self-talk" is something that I often hear mentioned in counseling circles. It's a phrase that isn't terribly difficult to figure out, yet I think it's unique enough to merit some explanation as we venture toward conquering its ability to influence our thinking.

"Self-talk" is the recording that plays over and over in our mind. It's the information that we tell ourselves repeatedly. It's the message that we remind ourselves of when we're trying to develop some level of perspective on our surroundings, circumstances and how we fit into the contexts that we find ourselves in.

Self-talk, in it's root form, doesn't necessarily need to be something negative. There are many occasions when our self-talk can be rather positive in nature. When you acknowledge in your mind that, "I'm having a good day," or "That person seems to like me," you're engaging in some level of positive self-talk. But in my experience, I haven't seen too many people make an appointment to speak with a counselor because they felt like they were struggling with too much "positivity" or because they weren't sure why they felt so "happy all the time."

One of the patterns I have observed in my roles as pastor, counselor and professor, is that many of the people who come to me for counsel or advice are struggling with a high degree of negative self-talk. They feel stuck and they often feel quite discouraged by it. Their minds swirl with a flood of negative thoughts about themselves and they typically suffer in silence for many years before doing something about it.

When a person is struggling with negative self-talk, their mind engages in a regular pattern of reminding them of a variety of negative things. Self-talk tends to be rather repetitive in nature. For starters, they will probably spend long periods of time dwelling on their **shortcomings**. In their mind, they will keep pointing out where they fell short of some perceived or arbitrary standard.

From there, they'll take some time to re-live and re-hash **past mistakes**. They'll go over the scenarios and the conversations that took place in their lowest moments. They'll remind themselves of just how embarrassed they felt at the time and then convince themselves that this is all other people think about when they're thinking of them.

Then they'll take some time to dwell on their **imperfections**. This may take place each morning as they look in the mirror and make preparation for the day. They'll dwell on the size of their nose or their complexion. They'll stare at their hair and wish something was different about it. They'll dwell on their size and tell themselves that they're too fat, short, oddly shaped, etc. Mind you that all these perceived imperfections are born from arbitrary standards of beauty and years of comparison.

When they aren't feeding their mind negative comments about their imperfections, they'll take some time to focus on their **limitations** - all the things that they wish they could know, do, experience, have, etc., but they don't have as of yet. They convince themselves that they will only experience happiness and true satisfaction once these limitations are eradicated.

Does any of this sound familiar to you? What does all of this illustrate? In essence, the bulk of our negative self-talk comes from adopting a worldly standard and worldly values as the primary standard through which we filter our thinking. Our negative self-talk is rooted in seeing ourselves and our circumstances from a fleshly perspective instead of from the perspective of our Lord. When we engage in this manner of thinking, we start to believe that temporary matters are eternal realities. And as is the case with all beliefs, our beliefs inform and influence our behaviors.

The beliefs that become ingrained in our minds because of our negative self-talk influence how we treat ourselves. If you continually repeat falsehoods and negative statements to yourself, you'll eventually begin to live out those statements. You'll treat yourself poorly. You'll give up on your goals. You'll stop striving in the areas in which God has gifted you to serve.

Your false beliefs will also impact how you react to others. Instead of conveying an example of faith and optimism in Christ, you'll convey a negative perspective. Instead of filtering criticism through the lens of what God's word says is true of you, you'll begin to agree with those who paint you with the brush of their destructive words. Instead of being patient with the weaknesses of others, you'll treat them harshly and impatiently because you've never learned how to be patient with yourself and your own weaknesses.

> *We who are strong have an obligation to bear with the failings of the weak, and not to please ourselves.* (**Romans 15:1**)

The sad reality of negative self-talk is that it really has a way of becoming your dominant perspective instead of a temporary nuisance. Once it's allowed to take root in your mind, it starts to spread to all areas of your thinking until it begins to dominate your worldview.

And the worst effect of it's growth is that it can (and often does) impact that way you start to see God. Instead of reminding yourself that He is the perfection of love, patience, forbearance, grace, mercy and compassion, you'll start seeing

Him through the same negative lens you see yourself. You'll begin thinking of Him in mean and angry terms. You'll tell yourself that the primary way He responds to you and His children is through harsh judgment and you'll completely forget that God delights in showing kindness toward His struggling children because it's His kindness that leads us toward repentance.

> *Or do you presume on the riches of his kindness and forbearance and patience, not knowing that God's kindness is meant to lead you to repentance?* **(Romans 2:4)**

But the Gospel of Jesus Christ is good news for weary souls. We may be adept at beating ourselves up and dragging ourselves down, but Jesus grants us His strength and He delights in redeeming our minds from a worldly and negative perspective.

Chapter 2.
What are the Long-term Affects of Negative Self-Talk?

Negative self-talk is something that all people engage in to some degree. But just because it's common, doesn't mean it's acceptable as a long-term strategy for living. Many people engage in some form of negative self-talk for years without ever addressing it or holding it up to the light of the gospel. They let it take root in their lives and as we stated in the previous chapter, it can become the dominant perspective through which they learn to see themselves and the world around them.

Some people are surrounded by a lot of negativity in general. Maybe you can identify with that reality. It's not uncommon to hear of people who struggle with a difficult boss at work or family member at home that conveys a high degree of negative emotion in their conversation and demeanor.

On top of that, in this era of social media and instant communication, we suffer from the "bad news travels fast" epidemic. It takes almost no time at all for bad news to travel around the world and some of us are feeding our minds a steady diet of bad news every waking hour of the day.

In my own case, I used to be a "news junkie." I would read and watch the news every chance I got. I enjoyed being up on everything that was taking place in the world and in my own country. But over time, I started to realize that being constantly bombarded with negative information (and to be honest, that's primarily what the daily news consists of), was having a bad emotional impact on me. It was fostering an elevated sense of worry and a desire to control things that I have absolutely no control over. When this became clear to me, I decided to scale back my consumption of news to about 10% of what it had been previously. I noticed an immediate improvement in how I felt.

But negative self-talk goes deeper than just the news we hear or the people we're surrounded with. While those things can contribute to the way we speak to and perceive ourselves, there's more to our concern than just our environment.

In future chapters, we will peel back some of these layers.

In the meantime, it's important to acknowledge that engaging in lengthy bouts of negative self-talk can produce measurable problems in our lives. What are some of these problems? What are some of the long-term effects of negative self-talk?

Physical Problems

Some of the more visible problems that may come about as the result of excessive and prolonged negative self-talk are physical in nature. It's interesting to note that frequently, we tend to dismiss a connection between what we believe and how our physical bodies are impacted by our beliefs, but researchers have often noted a correlation between the two.

Those who engage in high amounts of negative self-talk may begin to notice a **decline in motivation and energy levels**. So much of their mental energy is being poured into their daily battle with personal negativity that it may seem like they have very little energy for just about anything else. And if they're sufficiently discouraged, their motivation and ambition will likely suffer as well.

In some cases, people report developing hives, rashes and other **skin-related problems** when their thinking has been clouded by worry, fear and negativity. Others report struggling with **chronic levels of pain** that has no measurable connection to an infection or physical form of trauma.

Years ago I knew a man who was dealing with **abnormal heart rhythms** that began when he became overwhelmed with his life situation and began responding to the stress in his life from an unhealthy and negative perspective.

Very recently, I was speaking with a man who was struggling with **high blood pressure**. According to his physician, a major contributor to this abnormality was the worry and negativity that was taking root in his mind.

Researchers have also noted that prolonged negative self-talk can contribute to a **weakening of the immune system, greater susceptibility**

to illness, various digestive problems and difficulty sleeping.

This isn't a pretty picture, but physical problems aren't the only issues that can result from long-term exposure to negative self-talk.

Emotional Problems

In addition to physical problems, many people begin to experience unpleasant emotional changes after engaging in negative self-talk for lengthy periods of time. These emotional problems that begin to develop might not necessarily be immediately apparent to others, but their presence begins to be both felt and noticed over time.

One of the most common emotional problems to become apparent is **irritability**. Negative self-talk has a way of robbing most people of their joy which results in stronger feelings of irritation being expressed toward others.

Similarly, **anger issues** also tend to be present in the lives of those who engage in negative self-talk. Because they are angry with themselves, they often tend to over express their feelings of anger toward others. And if they're more adept at hiding those feelings, they may experience deep-seated **bitterness** as the fruit of their internalized anger.

One of the most serious emotional problems that can result from prolonged negative self-talk is **depression**. When we continually repeat a series of negative responses to ourselves for lengthy periods of time, we're essentially training our brains to operate negatively. This affects our mood and influences chemical reactions in our brains. Over time, this can lead to the induction of a lingering depressed state.

Spiritual Problems

As this pattern of experiencing physical and emotional problems continues, it eventually begins to spill over into our spiritual life and our daily walk with Christ. Because the message we're preaching to our hearts on a day-to-day basis is the antithesis of the truth of the Gospel, we begin to believe false gospels and we develop core beliefs that are out of line with God's word and His viewpoint toward His children. In coming chapters we'll examine this more closely, but at this point, let's observe some of the spiritual problems that may emerge.

In Christ, we receive **forgiveness**. He extends His pardon to all who trust in Him and receive His free gift of salvation. But followers of Christ who engage in unhealthy negative self-talk often forget that truth. They don't think of themselves as "forgiven". Because they spend much of their day judging themselves harshly, they begin to believe that God sees them primarily as objects of judgement, not as loved and forgiven children. And just as they struggle to see themselves as forgiven, they also tend to struggle to show forgiveness toward themselves and toward others.

In Christ, we have been shown **grace**. Though we weren't deserving of His favor, He has lavishly granted it toward all who call on His name. This is a truth that we are invited to delight in, but if our minds are swimming in the oppressive waters of negative self-talk, we tend to forget this truth. We stop showing grace to ourselves and we struggle to show it toward others.

In Christ, we have been granted **mercy**. In our sin, we deserved condemnation, but Jesus came and took our condemnation upon Himself at the cross then He rose from the grave in complete victory over sin, Satan and death. By nature, He is the perfection of mercy and He delights to show mercy toward His children. But maybe we struggle to accept that. And if we struggle to accept His mercy and won't show it to ourselves, we'll likely struggle to extend it toward others as well.

Negative self-talk doesn't just affect the way we think about ourselves. It eventually distorts our view of God and it damages the way we treat others. Negative self-talk isn't something that happens in a vacuum. It spreads from our cognition into our emotions, relationships and beliefs.

And, in my opinion, the worst part of it all is that it minimizes the Gospel of Jesus Christ in our lives. It affects our ability to live a life that is centered on Christ and His Gospel. It distorts the truth and we begin actively preaching a message to our hearts that is quite distant from the truth of the message of Jesus.

Notes: The Gilead Institute of America

JOHN STANGE

Chapter 3.
What is the Gospel?

As we mentioned in the previous chapter, engaging in a pattern of negative self-talk has the capacity to eventually alter our beliefs and distort or minimize the truth of the gospel in our lives.

It is my belief that the ultimate and most effective way to confront and overcome the lies of our negative self-talk is with the truth of the gospel. So then, what exactly is the gospel?

The word "gospel" literally means "good news." It is the good news of Jesus Christ and what He has accomplished to reconcile lost sinners who were distant from God into a close, abiding, eternal, family relationship with Him.

Looking back to Genesis, the first book of the Old Testament, we're told that God created mankind. He loved us and He made us unique. We are the only thing in His creation that has been created in His image and it has always been His desire that mankind would know Him deeply and personally.

> *26 Then God said, "Let us make man in our image, after our likeness. And let them have dominion over the fish of the sea and over the birds of the heavens and over the livestock and over all the earth and over every creeping thing that creeps on the earth."*
>
> *27 So God created man in his own image, in the image of God he created him; male and female he created them.*
>
> *28 And God blessed them. And God said to them, "Be fruitful and multiply and fill the earth and subdue it, and have dominion over the fish of the sea and over the birds of the heavens and over every living thing that moves on the earth." (**Genesis 1:26-28**)*

As wonderful as that sounds, that's not the way

many people in this world choose to live. In fact, we're told that man willfully and intentionally rebelled and sinned against God and therefore cut ourselves away from Him. Instead of delighting in a loving relationship with God, we chose to go our own way and we've been reaping the consequences ever since.

> *for all have sinned and fall short of the glory of God,* (**Romans 3:23**)

But God wasn't willing to let the story end there. Even though He would have been perfectly justified in casting us away from Him forever, He chose to do something about our distance. He wasn't willing to abandon us. He chose to give us a second chance.

By nature, God is the perfection of love. In His love, God sent His Son, Jesus Christ, to come to this earth to rescue humanity. Jesus is God in the flesh. The penalty for our sin was death and apart from God's miraculous intervention, we were doomed.

In love, Jesus took on flesh. He came to this earth and experienced a humble birth. He lived the perfect, sinless life that we could have never lived. He was executed by being crucified on a cross to pay for our sin, the righteous suffering the penalty that the unrighteous (us) deserved. Then He rose back to life on the third day after His execution. For His glory and for our benefit, His work accomplished the defeat of the power of sin, the power of death and Satan himself.

> *"For even the Son of Man came not to be served but to serve, and to give his life as a ransom for many." (**Mark 10:45**)*

> *And the Word became flesh and dwelt among us, and we have seen his glory, glory as of the only Son from the Father, full of grace and truth. (**John 1:14**)*

> *who was delivered up for our trespasses and raised for our justification. (**Romans 4:25**)*

It is His desire to share the victory that He secured over sin, Satan and death, with us. Jesus is the Savior of mankind and He offers us the only opportunity we could ever have to experience ultimate forgiveness of our sin. He calls us to repent of our unbelief and trust in Him alone for forgiveness. When we trust in Him, we are born again and made into a new creation, we are adopted into God's family, forgiven of our sin, declared holy in God's sight and granted the gift of eternal life in perfect, restored fellowship with Him forever.

*Therefore, if anyone is in Christ, he is a new creation. The old has passed away; behold, the new has come. (**2 Corinthians 5:17**)*

*But to all who did receive him, who believed in his name, he gave the right to become children of God, (**John 1:12**)*

"For God so loved the world, that he gave his only Son, that whoever believes in him should not perish but have eternal life."

(John 3:16)

This is exceedingly great news. There is no greater news that anyone could share. The fact that the God of the universe looked at us with compassion and lovingly chose to intervene into the mess we had created is utterly amazing. We rebelled against Him. We chose sin and death instead of perfection and life. We wanted nothing to do with God and were by nature, objects of His wrath. We deserved His judgement, yet He took the punishment we deserved upon Himself at the cross so that the penalty for our sin would be covered. He shows us mercy. He grants us grace. He loves us and He invites us to live in His love as objects of His mercy. Once we place our faith in Jesus Christ, this becomes our present day reality.

But let's be honest. This truth, even thought it is the greatest truth in the universe, is often quite far from our minds. We don't tend to think of ourselves as "loved" quite as often as we should. We don't think of ourselves as "objects of mercy", even though that's what we become the moment we trust in Jesus. We seem to prefer to think of ourselves from a very different perspective than what Scripture tells us is ultimately true of us in Christ.

We tell ourselves that we're unloved, unforgiven objects of wrath. Think about that for a second. Isn't that exactly what you're telling yourself when you engage in negative self-talk? We put ourselves down and we don't show ourselves much love, grace or mercy even though we are deeply loved by God. We think of ourselves as being objects of God's displeasure instead of realizing that when God the Father looks at us, He sees Jesus, God the Son, living inside us. And as the Father is pleased with the Son, so too is He pleased with us because we are, as Scripture says, "in Christ".

> *For we are his workmanship, created in Christ Jesus for good works, which God prepared beforehand, that we should walk in them.* (**Ephesians 2:10**)

What do you think your life would look like if you started to truly see yourself from God's perspective? What kind of impact do you think that would have on your overall thinking? How would your day-to-day life change if the truth of the gospel started to permeate the core of your beliefs? Do you suppose it would have an impact on the messages you preach to yourself? Do you think it might alter your pattern of negative self-talk? I do.

That's why we need to be reminded of these truths often. I frequently try to remind myself of who I truly am in Christ because even though I would like to be able to tell you that I never forget those truths, the fact of the matter is that sometimes, I get caught up in a worldly pattern of thinking and it can take me a little while before I start to realize this is happening to me.

I know I'm not the only one who experiences this. I have spent my entire adult life serving in pastoral ministry and the people I serve often tell me that they wrestle with this as well. In addition to my pastoral work, I direct a counseling practice and nearly every one of my clients have expressed some level of struggle with this. I also have the privilege of teaching several classes at a university near Philadelphia and many of my students are wrestling with this.   Likewise, my wife and my children also struggle in this area. We all do!

Not long ago, after my family went to sleep for the evening, I walked downstairs to my writing desk and put together a small book that lists 100 different things that the Bible tells us are true of us once we are in Christ. The next day, I sat down with my family and we started reading through it and the Scriptures that corresponded with each truth.   It was an encouraging experience for us all and a powerful reminder of the kind of truth that we all need to hear - the very truth that we frequently fail to remind ourselves of. *(If you're interested in reading it, the book is called "**Your Identity in Christ**").*

All this to say, the truth of the gospel should never be far from our minds. If it isn't on the forefront of our minds - informing our sense of identity and worldview, we will gravitate toward falsehoods that will cloud our thinking and perpetuate our pattern of engaging in negative self-talk.

God wants more for us than that. He wants the truth of His gospel to be part of all aspects of our lives, not just something that we relegate to a distant compartment in our mind.

In the next chapter, we are going to take a look at the difference between compartmentalizing the gospel and applying it to all aspects of our every day lives.

Chapter 4.
What is the difference between compartmentalizing the Gospel and applying it?

In most Christian contexts that I interact in, there is some level of understanding of the gospel. But one thing that has become increasingly clear to me is that many well-meaning Christians have an unfortunate habit of compartmentalizing the gospel. Instead of applying its deep and rich truths to all aspects of their lives, they tuck it away in a little box and don't seem to realize how this impacts their daily life and their walk with Christ.

In the previous chapter, we explained the message of the gospel and we identified its significance. As beautiful as these truths truly are, many Christians tend to think of the gospel as a "baby-step" or an "elementary truth" that eventually we need to move beyond if we're ever going to get to some of the deeper aspects of spiritual maturity.

Oddly enough, I have to confess that I have

noticed this pattern in my own life. For quite some time, if you asked me to explain the message of the gospel, I would have told you a little about Christ's plan of salvation and the discussion would have ended there. I didn't realize that I was compartmentalizing the gospel and I certainly didn't understand the fact that I was failing to comprehend the depth of its application.

In fact, I can distinctly remember attending a pastor's conference during my first year of full-time pastoral ministry and listening to the preaching of several speakers. I noticed a pattern among the speakers. They each made reference to the gospel in their preaching and to be honest, at the time, I started to grow annoyed with them. I remember thinking, "I came to this conference hoping to hear more than elementary teaching on the gospel. I was hoping that they'd get to the deeper stuff in Scripture." How unfortunate that my perspective was so limited and immature at the time.

The truth is, we are never called to go beyond the truth of the gospel. Rather, we're invited and encouraged to go deeper into it. We're encouraged to learn to apply it to all areas of our lives and to mirror the heart of Christ as the Holy Spirit empowers us to do so.

But for the longest time, I wanted to go beyond the gospel. In my thinking, the gospel was for other people. In particular, I considered it something that unbelievers needed, but not something that remained quite as relevant or necessary for genuine believers.

I was so wrong and as a result, I ended up preaching various "false gospels" to my heart on a daily basis. I didn't realize I was doing this, but this became my regular pattern. It's entirely possible that you may be doing the same thing to yourself as well. When the gospel is relegated to a small compartment in our lives, this is the inevitable outcome. We begin preaching a false gospel to ourselves and others, and our hearts drift toward functional saviors that are poor substitutions for the real thing, Jesus.

Preaching False Gospels

In practical terms, what does it look like to

preach a false gospel to your heart? A false gospel, at it's core, involves some form of works-based approval or some level of seeking worldly validation.

For instance, I became adept at preaching a works-based false gospel to my heart that taught that my life and reputation depended on my ministry success. I would drive myself to function at a level that was foolish and unhealthy. I said "yes" to every ministry opportunity that was presented to me and served on various boards and committees. I oversaw two primary ministries at the same time, rarely spent time at home and almost never took a day off or a vacation. Even though I had a wife and several children, I justified doing this because the work needed to be done and my job became an idol in my life.

I was burning myself out by doing this and in time, I started to resent some of my ministry obligations. By God's grace, I came to realize that I really needed to pull back from much of what I was doing, but I still hadn't yet identified that my actions were the fruit of a false, works-based gospel I had been preaching to my heart.

False gospels rest on a foundation of human effort. We give ourselves too much credit or we rely too heavily on our limited strengths. We gradually become less reliant on the Lord's power and we become overly dependent on our own wisdom and abilities. We try to carry burdens that we were never meant to carry and we wear ourselves out by demanding an inhuman level of performance from our mortal selves.

Now maybe you aren't quite as likely to take on as much responsibility as I tried to juggle as the fruit of the false gospels you've been preaching to your heart. But I'm guessing that if we poked and prodded at you long enough, we would find some areas where you're trying to carry burdens that Jesus wants to carry for you. I think we'd find some areas that you've been relying on your own strength and wisdom instead of the strength and wisdom of Christ.

For example, do you ever struggle with **fear or worry**? Fear has much to do with control. In fact, we tend to fear what we cannot control. We worry about circumstances that are out of our hands, partly because there's some part of us that wants to be in control of those situations. At times, we're not willing to fully trust in God to oversee our lives and control our circumstances.

This is an area where we frequently compartmentalize the gospel. The gospel reminds us that we don't need to fear because God is sovereign and He is working all things together for our good and His glory. The false gospel tells us that we need to be in control and furthermore, it convinces us that God might not be paying careful attention to our lives or that He might actually mess something up.

Let's look at another area where we might be compartmentalizing the gospel. How would you describe your **self-image**? Would you say it's generally healthy or generally poor? When someone asks you to tell them a little about yourself, how do you primarily describe yourself or define your existence?

A false gospel will tell you to think of yourself primarily through the lens of your abilities, possessions, talents, background, ethnicity, family background, education or location where you were born. But those are worldly priorities and aren't the criteria through which God sees and perceives you.

The gospel tells us that when we receive Christ's gift of salvation, we are made new creations in Christ. We are no longer who we once were. We're brand new. Our new identity is in Christ, not in our flesh. In Christ, we are loved, adopted, holy, family, redeemed, chosen, forgiven and so much more. But if we're preaching a false gospel to our hearts, we'll live as if this isn't true.

Or what about our **ability to relate to others**? Other people can be rather stressful at times. They can test our patience and incite our anger or displeasure. How does the message of the true gospel apply?

Since we have been shown love, mercy, grace, patience and forgiveness by Jesus, even though we deserved judgement and punishment, so too should we be eager to respond to others in like fashion. We're called to bear with the failings of others because that's the very thing Jesus has done for us.

> *We who are strong have an obligation to bear with the failings of the weak, and not to please ourselves.* *(Romans 15:1)*

Do you see where this is going? Are you starting to catch on? Can you see how compartmentalizing the gospel and preaching false gospels to our hearts can impact the degree to which we engage in negative self-talk?

Functional Saviors

In addition to false gospels, it would also be wise for us to note the presence of "functional saviors" as well because they have a profound impact on both our thinking and our behavior.

Functional saviors are things that we gravitate toward that we allow to take the place of Jesus in our lives. They are things or people that we believe can satisfy the ultimate longing of our hearts, apart from Christ.

Some people believe that a **spouse or children**

can satisfy their heart in ways that Christ can't. Even though spouses and children are wonderful things, they can never satisfy the longing of our souls like Jesus can, nor are they meant to.

Others believe that the **perfect career or level of income** can feed the deepest hunger of their hearts. But careers come and go and the love of money is at the root of much of the evil that is done in this world.

Some believe that **notoriety or praise** can produce more delight in their lives than Jesus. So they pursue fame or the applause of men. But people are fickle and the same people that sing your praises today can turn on you and abandon you tomorrow.

False gospels and functional saviors go hand-in-hand and both are the fruit of failing to apply the gospel to our daily lives. If we allow ourselves to believe that the gospel is merely a "baby-step" in our Christian life, we'll compartmentalize it instead of delving deeper into it and allowing the Holy Spirit to help us apply it more consistently to all areas of our living and thinking.

At the root of our negative self-talk, we will discover the presence of false gospels and functional saviors. Here's a few questions to wrestle with before we begin our next discussion.

1. How does the gospel teach me to receive criticism?

2. How does the gospel teach me to handle my less-than-perfect moments?

3. How does believing the gospel affect my outlook on the future?

4. What false gospels have I allowed myself to believe for far too long?

5. What functional saviors have I tried to rely on instead of seeking satisfaction for my soul through Jesus?

Take some time to ask yourself these questions before moving on to the next chapter. I believe it would be wise to pray and ask the Lord to grant you His wisdom so that you can grow in awareness of some of your blind spots as well as develop a deeper appreciation of His presence with you in the midst of your struggles. Once you have spent ample time in prayer and reflection, you'll be better prepared to move on to the next part of this book.

In the remaining chapters, I'm going to outline seven specific steps that I utilize in my own life and encourage others to utilize in theirs as they seek to overcome the power of negative self-talk with the truth of the gospel.

JOHN STANGE

Chapter 5.
Step One: Acknowledge your pain

At this point, I hope you have a working understanding of what negative self-talk is, where it finds its source and how it conflicts with the truth of the gospel. I believe that information is important to grasp if we're going to experience fruitful results from our attempts to overcome the presence of excessive negative self-talk in our lives.

With that foundation in place, now it's time to wrestle with what to do with that information. Beginning with this chapter and continuing through the remainder of this book, we are going to embark on a practical and intentional approach to utilizing the truth of the gospel to overcome the dominance of our personal negativity. And I think it all begins with humbly acknowledging our pain.

I don't know all the reasons why it is so, but for some reason, many Christians are under the impression that it is practically sinful for them to admit that they're hurting or struggling. I guess it's possible that we may be overly concerned with what others may think of us or maybe we're fearful that admitting our struggles might be evidence of a lack of faith on our part. But that's something we've got to be willing to move beyond if we're going to enjoy a reprieve from the torture we're putting ourselves through.

If we're going to walk in victory over the power of negative self-talk, we have to be honest about our pain. We have to acknowledge that it's there. God knows we're struggling. We know we're struggling. Others who are close to us may know it as well, but quite frequently, we're unwilling to fully admit it to ourselves. As a result, we prolong our pain and we dig our heels into the dirt of our struggle as if we're intent on remaining in it for the rest of our lives.

That's unfortunate, but it's common. Instead of acknowledging our pain and admitting to God and ourselves that it's real, we put on a happy face and we try our best to distract ourselves with our favorite forms of escape. We do anything we can to busy our minds or cause our thinking to drift from the struggles that cause us the most hurt.

Unfortunately, this just makes the problem worse. Instead of handling our hurt, we prolong it. We effectively nurture it and protect it until it becomes a constant presence in our lives. We think we're partially succeeding in avoiding it, but if we're truly honest with ourselves, we can see that we're actually living in the midst of our unresolved pain or grief every second of the day.

Is this the kind of life you want for yourself? Is this the kind of life you would wish on others? How long do you want to continue this charade? What lasting good do you think it's really accomplishing to live like this?

You don't have to pretend any longer. I realize that you may think that your struggles are so unique or that your pain is so different from what anyone else has, or is experiencing. Maybe you've convinced yourself that no one could ever understand what you're wrestling with, but that simply isn't true. If you want to work through your struggle, you need to acknowledge that it's real. Living in a pretend world is just an escape. It's just a fantasy and deep down, you already know that it's not working anyway.

> *No temptation has overtaken you that is not common to man. God is faithful, and he will not let you be tempted beyond your ability, but with the temptation he will also provide the way of escape, that you may be able to endure it.*
> *(1 Corinthians 10:13)*

Have you ever taken a moment to admit and confess your struggles to God? Would that be too painful to consider? Do you suppose He would understand or is there a part of your belief system (aka, the false gospels you have tried to rely on) that expects God to condemn you and treat you harshly because you're struggling?

One of the most amazing things about our God is that we worship a Creator who truly understands what we're wrestling with. During the earthly ministry of Jesus, He experienced all aspects of life in this world. Hunger.

Disappointment. Betrayal. Insult. Injury. Sorrow. Temptation. Jesus experienced it all and although He never sinned, He can sympathize with our weaknesses. He understands our struggles. He knows what we're wrestling with because He's walked a mile in our shoes. He subjected Himself to experiencing life like we experience life and He feels compassion for us as we're in the midst of our low seasons.

> *For we do not have a high priest who is unable to sympathize with our weaknesses, but one who in every respect has been tempted as we are, yet without sin.* (***Hebrews 4:15***)

Jesus doesn't expect you to pretend. He doesn't expect you to put on a happy face all the time nor does He want you to try to convince everyone you know that you're fine when you aren't. He invites you to be real and transparent with Him. He invites you to be honest. He invites you to trust Him with your burdens.

> *Come to me, all who labor and*

are heavy laden, and I will give
*you rest. (**Matthew 11:28**)*

Does the gospel you preach to yourself present Jesus as open-armed or closed-fisted toward you? Does the gospel you preach to yourself communicate Christ's invitation to come to Him or are you effectively telling yourself that God doesn't want anything to do with you because your pain is too deep or your problems are too severe?

It's time to take off the mask. It's time to stop playing games with yourself. Now is the time for honesty. What is the source of your pain? Where are you hurting? Why are you hurting? How are you hurting?

When I was a child, my parents would encourage me to clean my room. But that's not a task most children are terribly fond of. Like most children, my solution to the problem was to take my toys and laundry and stuff them under my bed, in closets or in drawers. To the casual observer, I'm sure my room looked moderately clean, but the truth was that the mess was still there. It was just hidden.

Hiding your mess doesn't make it go away. It just makes it less visible. And while it's being disguised, it's given more of an opportunity to stick around even longer.

The first step to overcoming our negative self-talk is to finally acknowledge our pain. The time for hiding it has come to an end. It's time to be honest with ourselves and honest with God.

So, what is it? Where do you hurt the most? Bring this before the Lord in prayer. Trust Him with your admission. He invites you with open arms to finally come to Him with the burden you've been trying to carry. A burden that's too heavy for you, but certainly isn't too heavy for Him.

JOHN STANGE

Chapter 6.
Step Two: Examine your beliefs

After we acknowledge our pain and permit ourselves to admit that it's real, it's time to peel another layer of our struggle away. It's time for us to carefully examine our beliefs.

In life, behavior follows belief. Everything we do is directly connected to what we believe is true. We eat because we believe (or have faith) that food will curb our hunger. We wash our hands because we believe it is a healthy way to stop the spread of germs and prevent illness. We fertilize our gardens because we believe it will provide nutrients to our plants.

In the spiritual realm, we pray because we believe that God answers prayer. We share our faith in Christ because we believe that trusting in Jesus is the key to receiving His gift of eternal life. We fellowship with a local church because we believe it helps strengthen our faith and provides a network of support, encouragement and accountability. Our actions are the fruit of our convictions. Our behaviors are the visible testimony of our core convictions.

That being said, please take a moment to ask yourself this question, *"What are my core beliefs about life, purpose and God Himself?"* It may be difficult to answer this question right away, but it's definitely healthy to examine your deeply held beliefs because they are directly influencing what you choose to do.

I was recently speaking with someone who admitted that he craves the approval of others. He wants others to think well of him and he alters his behavior and sacrifices his preferences to gain acceptance.

In the midst of our conversation, I asked Him to complete this sentence, *"A truly happy life depends on ..."* He thought for a minute and then replied, *"A truly happy life depends on being accepted by others."*

This was a significant moment for him. It was difficult for him to make this admission, but I could see that it was a relief to finally bring out in the open something that was a guarded secret that produced shame and fostered insecurity in his life. This was his core belief and unfortunately, it was proving to be a poor foundation for him to build his life on.

Not long ago, I was speaking with a woman who is extremely critical of herself. She pushes herself very hard and she tries to operate at a very high level, every single day of her life. She rarely takes breaks, but every few months, she comes to a crashing point where she feels like she hits a wall and she crumbles within herself.

She's particularly harsh on herself when she makes a mistake. While she's willing to admit her mistakes, she always does so with a great degree of pain. It's as if she believes in those moments that life as she knows it is over once her mistakes, even the small ones, are brought out into the open. She feels devastated and treats herself poorly over things that would seem minor to just about any outside observer.

When I asked her to answer the question, *"A truly happy life depends on ..."*, she replied, *"A truly happy life depends never making mistakes."* Because she believed this at the core of her being, she felt like she had no ability to process her less than stellar moments. If she believed that she had failed to meet her impossible standard, she would castigate herself and convince herself that she was completely unloved by people and practically unloved by God.

So how would you answer the same question? What are you core beliefs? What do you believe a truly satisfying life depends on?

As you answer this question through the lens of the gospel, you're likely to discover the presence of false gospels and functional saviors within your belief system. Were you able to identify their presence in the belief systems of the people I just mentioned?

In the first example, you have a man who believed that his life depended on the acceptance and approval of others. He was willing to make major life changes in order to live up to the arbitrary standards of others, provided that they gave him some level of assurance that they approved of him.

This man was a believer in Christ. If he was viewing himself through the lens of the gospel, he would have already accepted the fact that in God's eyes, he was accepted and welcomed into God's family. In fact, he would have acknowledged that he had been intentionally adopted by God, was chosen before the foundation of the earth, and had been granted an eternal inheritance in Christ's kingdom. But it seems that he was struggling to fully believe that, and his behaviors were the fruit of his beliefs.

> *Blessed be the God and Father of our Lord Jesus Christ, who has blessed us in Christ with every spiritual blessing in the heavenly places, 4 even as he chose us in him before the foundation of the world, that we should be holy and blameless before him. In love 5 he predestined us for adoption as sons through Jesus Christ, according to the purpose of his will, 6 to the praise of his glorious grace, with which he has*

blessed us in the Beloved.
(Ephesians 1:3-6)

In the second example, you have a woman who tries to be a perfectionist. While she knows she's a sinner by nature, she struggles to come to terms with that fact because she equates imperfections in character with rejection. Instead of grieving over her sin in a healthy and redemptive manner, she completely catastrophizes her admission of her struggles.

Even though she professes to have faith in Christ, she is forgetting the essence of the gospel. She is forgetting the fact that Jesus Himself told us that He came, not to rescue the healthy, but to heal the sick. He alone is perfect and the good news is that in the eyes of God, we are likewise seen as being holy and blameless because by faith, we are reckoned as being in Christ.

> *And when Jesus heard it, he said to them, "Those who are well have no need of a physician, but those who are sick. I came not to call the righteous, but sinners."*

64

(Mark 2:17)

But that's not how she most often sees herself. She was overly harsh on herself because deep down, she believed that life depended on being perfect. She was trying to live her life as if she could be her own savior and didn't have the need for Jesus to be perfect for her.

Does any of this sound familiar to you? Is any of this reminiscent of some of the core beliefs you wrestle with? Can you see the correlation between our beliefs and our behaviors?

Identifying what you truly believe is critical if you're going to overcome the dominance of your negative self-talk. I believe that negative self-talk is one of the primary tools Satan likes to use in order to discourage God's people. He doesn't want you dwelling on the fact that you were created in God's image. He doesn't want you to think of yourself as loved. He doesn't want you to be gracious or forgiving to yourself. Rather, he wants you to wallow in your perceived weaknesses and struggles. He wants you to repeat a mantra to yourself of the false gospels that are 100% dependent on human effort (and therefore ineffective). He wants you to beat yourself up and crush your spirit. He wants you to see your life through a lens of bitterness and self-degradation.

But Christ desires more and better things for you than that. He wants to be at the core of your beliefs. He wants to be at the center of your convictions. He wants you to start to see yourself, your circumstances and this world through the lens of His loving eyes.

By His grace, He invites you to bring to light the false beliefs that have been influencing your behavior and informing the message you've been preaching to your heart. He invites you to delight in Him and stop feeding yourself a steady diet of lies and distortions that crumble when held up to the light of His truth.

Chapter 7.
Step Three: Identify what you say to yourself

The third step in this process is to take some time, even if it's somewhat difficult and painful in the moment, to begin to identify what you say to yourself. What is the content of the message you've been preaching to your heart? What message have you been reinforcing in your brain through regular repetition?

For some people, this can be a particularly difficult step. It isn't comfortable to intentionally think about the negative self-talk that you communicate to yourself. But I believe that if we allow it to continue to operate in secret, without exposing it to the light, we're going to continue to experience the pain of leaving it unaddressed.

To help you identify the negative self-talk that you repeat to yourself, it may be helpful to begin with identifying a particularly discouraging, difficult or embarrassing moment in your recent past.

* When was the last time someone insulted you or hurt your feelings?

* When was the last time you experienced failure at a task or goal that you set for yourself?

* When was the last time you made a mistake or had a lapse in judgement that resulted in you feeling shame or embarrassment?

Do you have a particular event in mind? I realize that it's probably not enjoyable to think about it, but at the same time, it can be genuinely beneficial when we learn to view our experiences through the redemptive lens of Christ's gospel.

Now that you've identified a difficult moment that triggered your negative self-talk, it's time to catalogue some of the things that you regularly tell yourself. The ironic thing about this is that, in the moment, you probably believe that you're the only one behaving this way, but if you could journey to a public place and see speech bubbles over peoples' heads, I think you would be surprised at just how common this behavior tends to be. Many of us are telling ourselves some very negative things on a very regular basis and our comments tend to fall into predictable patterns or categories.

My guess is that your negative self-talk might resemble some of these statements:

* *"I am terrible at this."*

* *"I mess everything up."*

* *"I'm not good at anything."*

* *"I'm the worst parent ever."*

* *"I'm a terrible spouse."*

* *"I'm a total failure at life."*

* *"My faith is so weak."*

* *"I'm such a hypocrite."*

* *"I must be the worst Christian."*

* *"I'm terrible at my job and I wouldn't blame my boss for firing me."*

* "Everyone must think poorly of me."
* "My life is totally messed up."
* "It would be easier to be dead than to have to keep living my terrible life."
* "Everyone hates me."
* "No one respects me."
* "I look terrible."
* "I'm not very smart."
* "I have nothing meaningful to contribute to this conversation."
* "I'm embarrassed that I don't have more money."
* "There is always someone who can accomplish just about anything better than I can."
* "My life has been a total waste."
* "I will never do anything that's truly meaningful."

* *"God must be punishing me."*

* *"God doesn't love me, and I don't blame Him because I don't even love myself."*

I could keep listing more examples of negative self-talk, but I think this list covers most of the major areas. We beat ourselves up over our mistakes, our history, our status, our relationships, our appearance, our accomplishments and our walk with God. When we're anything less than perfect in any area of our life, we start catastophizing and convincing ourselves that our whole world is falling apart and everyone, including God, must hate us.

Yikes! That's a pretty heavy load to try and bear. What a painful message to pound into the fabric of our hearts. It's no wonder we feel like garbage. We're feeding our minds and hearts a steady stream of lies, but we're believing these falsehoods and then living our lives as if they're true.

Wouldn't it be nice to be free from this

destructive cycle? Wouldn't it be nice to wake up each day, confident in the truth of who we are in Jesus and refreshed by the truth of His gospel instead of lies that find their source in worldly and ungodly thinking?

We aren't the first Christians to struggle with worldly thinking. I appreciate the Apostle Paul's challenge to the Corinthian church in the books of 1 & 2 Corinthians. The Corinthian Christians were unfortunately known for their worldly thinking. Even though their faith in Christ got off to a good start when they first believed the gospel, over time, they started welcoming worldly thinking back into their lives and it was resulting in a great amount of division in their church.

People were fighting each other and suing each other in the courts. Leaders were being disrespected. Hearts were becoming greedy. Immoral behavior was being condoned. The Corinthians are a good example of how behavior tends to follow belief and their beliefs were certainly being impacted by their acceptance of worldly values.

I appreciate Paul's words to them in 1 Corinthians 3:

> *18 Let no one deceive himself. If anyone among you thinks that he is wise in this age, let him become a fool that he may become wise. 19 For the wisdom of this world is folly with God. For it is written, "He catches the wise in their craftiness," 20 and again, "The Lord knows the thoughts of the wise, that they are futile." 21 So let no one boast in men. For all things are yours, 22 whether Paul or Apollos or Cephas or the world or life or death or the present or the future—all are yours, 23 and you are Christ's, and Christ is God's.* (**1 Corinthians 3:18-23**)

Our battle with negative self-talk resembles the struggle that was taking place in Corinth. Instead of valuing the wisdom of the Holy Spirit, they esteemed the wisdom of man over the wisdom of God.

Just think for a moment about the values that are present in what we're telling ourselves. We're reinforcing a belief that our value is not based on who we are in Christ. Rather, we're telling ourselves that we only have value if what we do, what we have and how we look measures up to worldly standards and worldly ambitions.

Take a moment if you would, and write out a list of what you tell yourself in your lowest moments. Your list might have some resemblance to the list I suggested or it might include other comments that are more unique and individualized. Before reading any further, please jot your list down, even if you're only able to come up with a few short statements.

--

What's it like to look at this list? Stare at it for just a moment. How does it feel to see it written out on paper?

What are some of the worldly values that you can identify in your statements of negative self-talk? Are you someone who bases your sense of worth on your appearance? Is your value being based on what you do? Is your hope being placed in what you own? Do you disparage your existence because you're stuck dwelling on your past mistakes? Do you care more about what you think your peers think about you than what God thinks about you? Are you unwilling to accept that God's love is based on His very nature, not our performance, and is shared unconditionally with His children?

These are important questions to ask and I hope the Holy Spirit is using them to trigger deeper understanding in your heart as to what is really motiving your negative self-talk.

Keep the list of your negative self-talk handy and take some time to identify and write down any additional statements that come to mind. What else are you saying to yourself that isn't on this list yet? Ask the Lord to show it to you, then jot it down when He does so. Again, I realize that these aren't pleasant sentences to stare at, but this list is going to be helpful to have on hand as we move along into the next step of the process of overcoming negative self-talk with the truth of the gospel.

Chapter 8.
Step Four: Repeat it to someone you love

The Lord has blessed me with four children. I love being a father. It's a role that's filled with demands, sacrifices, joy and blessing. I'm thankful to have the privilege to guide and mold many aspects of the lives of my children.

I take my responsibility as their father very seriously. I'm mindful of the fact that they currently make and will continue to make major life decisions based on my influence and instruction. As I observe this playing out in their lives, it has made me even more conscious of the way that I speak to them and the information I share with them. I'm aware that their lives and beliefs are often being shaped by what they hear from me.

Words are powerful things. Scripture cautions us to be careful in their use.

> *7 For every kind of beast and bird, of reptile and sea creature,*

*can be tamed and has been tamed by mankind, 8 but no human being can tame the tongue. It is a restless evil, full of deadly poison. 9 With it we bless our Lord and Father, and with it we curse people who are made in the likeness of God. 10 From the same mouth come blessing and cursing. My brothers, these things ought not to be so. (**James 3:7-10**)*

I want my children, and anyone I interact with, to experience encouragement and edification from my words. I want the Lord to use my words to build people up and foster peace among the family of God. But I can testify, as can we all, that there are many times when I have fallen far short of that ideal.

I'm so thankful that the Lord isn't flippant in the ways He chooses to communicate with us. Even though we deserve the full force of His wrath, He has elected to communicate to our hearts in such a way that we can experience the warmth of His kindness and love.

Or do you presume on the riches of his kindness and forbearance and patience, not knowing that God's kindness is meant to lead you to repentance? (**Romans 2:4**)

Take my yoke upon you, and learn from me, for I am gentle and lowly in heart, and you will find rest for your souls. (**Matthew 11:29**)

Following Christ's gracious example, I try to model His heart in my manner of communication. For this reason, it grieves my heart when it becomes apparent to me that there are times when my words have been less than gracious. I do not enjoy hurting others with what I say and I'm guessing you probably feel the same way.

So why do we hurt ourselves the way we do by communicating hurtful falsehoods to our hearts with the internal repetition of negative self-talk? Why do we speak to ourselves in a way that doesn't model Christ's heart? Why do we speak to ourselves in a way that doesn't resemble how we speak to our children (or does it)? Why do we speak to ourselves in a way that doesn't typify the way we speak to people in general? What makes negative self-talk so permissible and common to us?

I'm guessing that if you could just snap your fingers and make yourself stop talking this way to yourself, you would do so. But as we well know, the process of overcoming long-held practices doesn't typically work like that.

Still, it's important that something constructive be done about this. Having first acknowledged our pain, examined our beliefs and identified what we say, I would like to suggest a fourth step in overcoming the grip of negative self-talk. **Take your list and repeat it to someone you love**.

Before you follow through with that, let me clarify that thought a little bit. Usually, for us to break habits that have gripped us for lengthy periods of time, we need to begin to see them from a brand new perspective. **Our beliefs**

toward these habits and their role in our lives needs to change and sometimes, we need something more drastic and out of the ordinary to jolt us into making that change. Verbalizing your negative self-talk to a trusted family member, forcing yourself to hear it out loud and see the look on their face as you do so, might be just the kind of jolt you need.

As crazy as this idea might sound, I have seen this process work, first hand, in multiple counseling environments. But just the same, it's important to begin by selecting the right person to partner with you in this experiment. Likewise, you'll need their help later on when we progress to the seventh step of this process.

Who do you know that you feel like you can trust with your major struggles and concerns? Who has the Lord placed in your life that has shown that they are more than willing to sacrifice their time to sit with you in the midst of your mess and patiently work with you as you wrestle with your concerns? Do you have a spouse, sibling or friend that might be willing to walk through this process with you? *(Note: I would be hesitant to request the help of your children with this kind of task, even if they are adults.)*

Once you've identified someone who would be willing to partner with you in this intervention, take a moment to be transparent with them about your struggle. Let them know about the battle that's been taking place in your mind. Share about how this has been affecting your self-perception, motivation and relationship with God. Ask their permission to give them a full view and an inside look at what you've been dealing with.

If they are comfortable with doing so, let them know that you are going to repeat the statements you've identified on your list in such a way that they are directed toward them. Tell them that you need to force yourself to hear these statements spoken out loud and you need to see a facial picture of what it looks like when a heart is on the receiving end of these words. Then work through your list.

If you tell yourself that you're a failure, tell your friend, *"You're a failure."*

If you tell yourself that your mistakes are what define you, tell your friend, *"You should be ashamed of yourself."*

If you tell yourself that you are unattractive, tell your friend, *"You look terrible. You're an ugly person."*

If you tell yourself that your worth is measured by what you own or possess, tell your friend, *"You're poor and you're always going to be poor."*

Walk through each part of your list and speak those negative statements to your friend who has volunteered to help you. Look them in the eye as you repeat each word. Emphasize each statement with the same inflection you use when you say these things to yourself. Let your ears hear these hurtful words and allow your eyes to witness the measure of their impact on your friend's face.

Odds are, this will be difficult to do. These will be difficult statements to repeat and it may be quite painful for your compassionate friend to hear you say these things, knowing that this is the script that runs through your mind each day.

Once you finish sharing your list, take some time to debrief. Ask your friend what they think about what you shared and how they were impacted emotionally by having to receive these hurtful statements. Then mourn together. Grieve the fact that these are the kinds of words that have clouded your thinking for far too long. Grieve the fact that you've been drilling your soul with statements that bear no likeness to the liberating and loving truth of the gospel of Jesus Christ.

Give yourself permission to grieve. It's good for the heart and it will help you to acknowledge the sorrow you've been bottling up for so many years based on the false gospels you've been preaching to your heart.

> *Frustration is better than laughter, because a sad face is good for the heart.*
> *(Ecclesiastes 7:3, NIV)*

Chapter 9.
Step Five: Identify the source of your negative self-talk

As we mentioned in the previous chapter, the experience of verbalizing one's negative self-talk to someone else can be rather jarring and uncomfortable. It usually prompts some level of grief and it helps to clarify just how destructive this habit can truly be.

Once that's understood, it's helpful to take a step back for a day or so for some meaningful reflection and soul-searching. By this point, you're probably not treating your negative self-talk as a harmless nuisance. You're coming to see it as it really is - a distortion of the gospel and a contradiction to how you're truly viewed in God's eyes.

With this new perspective activated, it's time to dig a little into your life in an attempt to discern where your negative self-talk is rooted. Why do you think this way? When did you first start thinking like this? What prompted this form of mental response and self-perception?

Each of us has a unique life story, but even in the midst of the uniqueness of our experiences, there are also common patterns in our lives. Somewhere along the way, your propensity to engage in negative self-talk was stimulated. Somewhere along the way, you were influenced to start seeing yourself the way you do. Somewhere along the way, your tendency to view yourself and your life through the lens of a false gospel was reinforced.

Take a moment right now to think about your life. Keep walking backward in time through the years you've lived. Remind yourself of all your significant experiences and major life influences. Who did you interact with? What was the interaction like? How did people talk to you? What happened to you that was outside of your control?

Several years ago I was counseling an older woman who had engaged in debilitating negative self-talk for years. In fact, this was something she had engaged in for the entirety of her adult life as well as her teenage and adolescent years.

She was struggling with obesity and other health concerns. She didn't like herself very much. She hated how she looked in the mirror. She repeatedly told herself that she would never succeed in life and she held herself back from doing many things she would have genuinely enjoyed.

She wasn't married and didn't believe any man could ever truly love her enough to marry her, but she did have a son with a man when she was in her mid-20's. Because he was willing to show her some interest and attention, she gave in to his advances and was intimate with him. When he learned she was pregnant, he abandoned her and left her to raise their son alone. This experience strongly reinforced her belief that she was unattractive and unlovable.

When I asked her to delve a little deeper into her past and share about her family, she told me about her very dysfunctional home life as a child. Her mother passed away when she was less than two years old and her aunt moved in with her family to help care for her siblings and her. Her father worked regularly, but he had a very passive personality and he often gave in to his addiction to alcohol.

Her aunt (who was her father's older sister), tried her best to be motherly at first. She showed a lot of favor to this woman's brothers, but over time came to resent the fact that she was helping to care for children that she didn't truly consider her own. She also resented the fact that their father was often drunk and not very helpful with most household responsibilities.

In time, this aunt became physically abusive to the father. She would hit him, slap him and kick him. He never retaliated physically, but would do his best to spend as much time away from the home as possible. When he was home, she would yell at him and severely criticize him in front of his children.

This woman resented the fact that she was living in a situation she felt stuck in. She agreed to live with her brother and his children because she was financially struggling to live by herself, but now she felt stuck in a situation that no longer appealed to her.

In her anger, she became verbally abusive to her niece. She told her she was ugly. She made her think that she smelled bad. She was regularly told that she was overweight. She was criticized for her inability to find a boyfriend. Her intelligence was demeaned and in general, she grew up feeling terrible about herself.

As we were sitting in my office talking about this, I could tell that the source of her negative self-talk was becoming obvious to this woman. In fact, when I asked her what the voice in her head sounded like, she said, *"It sounds just like my aunt!"* Then she broke down and wept.

It was a difficult experience for her to re-live some of these experiences, but it was instructive as we tried to get to the bottom of why she felt so poorly about herself and why she constantly engaged in such negative dialogues in her mind.

Have you ever tried walking down the difficult road this woman was willing to journey on? Have you ever tried to trace when your pattern of negative self-degradation began? Have you tried to identify a connection between what you tell yourself and the experiences of your past?

I know a man who was regularly bullied when he was in elementary school. He came from a loving family, but his classmates were merciless in their treatment of him for years. He has always struggled to move beyond their insults.

I know a woman who grew up blaming herself for her parents' divorce. She never married because she's concerned that she'll "*ruin that marriage as well.*"

What do you suppose might be influencing you to think the way you do? What is the source of your self-talk?

Let me suggest several options that you might want to explore. The first being your **past experiences**. Our life experiences have a major impact on how we see ourselves and others. They influence us to respond to new life experiences in similar ways. How have you been shaped by what you've endured in the past?

Another avenue to look at are the **people** who

had the opportunity to influence you at impressionable stages of your life. How did they speak to you? How did they treat you? Were they gracious and encouraging to you or were you regularly demeaned or verbally abused?

Something else that's important to consider is **Satan himself**. Scripture reveals that he takes pleasure in hurting people, bringing accusation against them, and influencing them to believe falsehoods about this world, themselves and God.

> *Be sober-minded; be watchful. Your adversary the devil prowls around like a roaring lion, seeking someone to devour.* (*1 Peter 5:8*)

> *Now the Spirit expressly says that in later times some will depart from the faith by devoting themselves to deceitful spirits and teachings of demons,* (*1 Timothy 4:1*)

And I heard a loud voice in heaven, saying, "Now the salvation and the power and the kingdom of our God and the authority of his Christ have come, for the accuser of our brothers has been thrown down, who accuses them day and night before our God. **(Revelation 12:10)**

One other source of false gospels and negative self-talk is unfortunately, **ourselves**. By nature, we struggle with sin and can easily begin to cloud our own minds with false beliefs and faulty world views when our thinking becomes rooted in the values and priorities of this world. The longer we value what this world values over what Christ values, the more we're opening ourselves up to a pattern of thinking that does not typify the loving heart of Christ.

Do not love the world or the things in the world. If anyone loves the world, the love of the Father is not in him. **(1 John 2:15)**

After contemplating these options, what do you believe may be the primary source of your negative self-talk? Is it rooted in your past experiences? Has it been reinforced by hurtful people? Is Satan bringing accusation against you? Is your heart captivated and clouded by the things of this world?

Maybe after looking at these options, you can identify several potential sources of your negative self-talk. That's entirely likely. You may have one or two sources that are primary in significance, but it's quite possible that there are multiple sources that have fed the unhelpful and regularly discouraging conversation that's taking place in your mind.

Now that you've identified some of these sources, what's next? Well, the next step is my favorite step of all. It's a step that refreshes my soul and is the fruit of Christ's power to renew our minds.

But that is not the way you learned Christ!— 21 assuming that you have heard about him

and were taught in him, as the truth is in Jesus, 22 to put off your old self, which belongs to your former manner of life and is corrupt through deceitful desires, 23 and to be renewed in the spirit of your minds, 24 and to put on the new self, created after the likeness of God in true righteousness and holiness.
(Ephesians 4:20-24)

Chapter 10.
Step Six: Meditate on the truth of the Gospel

When negative self-talk becomes our daily pattern and a primary drainer of our mental energy, it can likewise remain at the forefront of our thinking. It can cloud our beliefs and rob us of the fullness of the experience of delighting in Christ throughout the course of our day.

But this is not Christ's desire for those who are part of His family. He desires that we experience and live in the fullness of the freedom that we have in Him. This also includes the fact that our old way of thinking has been robbed of the power it once had over us. We no longer need to think and believe according to a worldly and defeated standard. Scripture tells us we have been given the "mind of Christ."

> *"For who has understood the mind of the Lord so as to instruct him?" But we have the mind of Christ.* **(1 Corinthians 2:16)**

The blessing of having "the mind of Christ" is a gift of the grace of God granted to all believers. We have been blessed with the unique privilege to begin seeing things like Christ sees things. We can see ourselves from His perspective. We can view others from His perspective. We can view our circumstances from His perspective. This is an amazing truth, but how often do we live as if this is true?

So often, even though God has revealed His plans and perspective to us in His word, we live as if they are a complete mystery. Even though He impresses the truth of His will to our minds through the still small voice of the Holy Spirit, we have a habit of spending our days believing that the opposite of the gospel is what is most true of us. Instead of finding rest for our souls in Jesus, we live as if our hearts will only find peace through what this world can offer us.

And with that as our perspective, we spend a considerable amount of time dwelling on things that are not of God. We fill our minds with all kinds of worries and "what if" scenarios. We judge ourselves harshly for our mistakes and even though we tell others that God is gracious and merciful, we resist reflecting His grace and mercy toward ourselves. We dwell on earthly things. We constantly criticize ourselves instead of preaching the gospel to our thirsty hearts.

But Christ wants more for us than that. He didn't come to this earth, live a perfect life, die a brutal death and rise from the grave in victory, just for us to live like we're in a constant state of defeat. He wants us to dwell on the victory He has secured on our behalf and live with confidence in Him because He who defeated sin, Satan and death is alive within us and He wants our hearts and our minds to focus on seeking things that are above instead of becoming stuck in the mire of this earth's muddy soil.

> *If then you have been raised with Christ, seek the things that are above, where Christ is, seated at the right hand of God. 2 Set your minds on things that are above, not on things that are on earth. 3 For you have died, and your life*

*is hidden with Christ in God. 4
When Christ who is your life
appears, then you also will
appear with him in glory.
(Colossians 3:1-4)*

How much of your thinking is focused on
eternal matters? Do you remind yourself of
eternal truth or consume yourself with
temporary issues? Is your mind set on things
that are above or are you still keeping yourself
entrenched in the very things Jesus rescued you
from? Do you believe the same things He
believes or is what He communicated too good
to possibly be true or too distant to possibly be
relevant to your life at present?

One of the most refreshing things we can do is
to think on things that are above. Sometimes I
need to remind myself of **Colossians 3:2** just
before I go to sleep in the evening. I don't
know why, but my mind seems dwell on earthly
things and earthly worries most noticeably just
before I'm trying to go to bed. All the things I
have been allowing myself to worry about seem
to come to the surface at that time of day. All
my heaviest concerns (the concerns that I'm

trying to handle in my own strength without giving them over to the Lord) tend to emerge and dominate my thinking right when I'm trying to quiet down and settle in for a nice rest.

When does your negative self-talk tend to become most pronounced? When does it seem to become most active? In those moments and as much as possible throughout our day, we need to engage in a more Spirit-led exercise. Instead of dwelling on our worries and unreleased burdens, we need the Spirit's help to dwell on things above. We need to regularly meditate on the truth of the gospel.

Meditating on the truth of the gospel is not a natural exercise and as such, it may not necessarily be something you find particularly easy to do at first. Our natural inclination and the pattern many of us have engaged in for most of our life is to think on earthly things. We're harsh and critical with ourselves. We're unforgiving and we keep a record of our mistakes. We try to carry burdens that we are completely incapable of lifting on our own.

But meditating on the truth of the gospel is

nourishing and encouraging to our weary souls. As we do so, the Lord helps us not to compartmentalize His gospel and we begin to experience just how relevant His truth is to us in all aspects of our lives.

So, practically speaking, what does it look like to meditate or dwell on the truth of the gospel throughout the course of our day?

For starters, I think it's important for us to **take some time to dwell on who God is and what His nature is like**. What does He reveal to us about Himself? Why does He love us like He does? What is His plan for His creation? How does He facilitate this plan?

I could list answers to these questions, but the truth is, you can easily answer these questions by reading the pages of Scripture. It very well may be that one of the contributing factors to the presence of negative self-talk in your life is your lack of familiarity with what the Lord has revealed in the Bible. What difference do you think it would make if you started off each day by reading just one chapter of the Bible? It usually takes about 5 minutes to read one chapter. Sometimes less. Is that something you have time for at the start of your day?

God's word reveals to us that He is all-knowing, all-powerful and present everywhere at once. He is the perfection of love. He is the perfection of mercy. He is the perfection of grace. He is the perfection of compassion and He delights in giving good things to His children. Do you believe this?

God's word also reveals to us that though our hearts like to seek satisfaction and peace through worldly and temporary sources, our hearts will only find the satisfaction and peace that we need through Jesus.

> *Jesus said to her, "Everyone who drinks of this water will be thirsty again, 14 but whoever drinks of the water that I will give him will never be thirsty again. The water that I will give him will become in him a spring of water welling up to eternal life."* (**John 4:13-14**)

> *do not be anxious about anything,*

> *but in everything by prayer and
> supplication with thanksgiving let
> your requests be made known to
> God. 7 And the peace of God,
> which surpasses all
> understanding, will guard your
> hearts and your minds in Christ
> Jesus.* **(Philippians 4:6-7)**

As we dwell on the message of the gospel, we begin to realize that Christ's desire for us is that we learn to trust Him. That we stop placing our confidence in what we can accomplish or control and learn to rest in the fact that He's got our best interest at heart and is working all things together for our good and His glory.

> *And we know that for those who
> love God all things work together
> for good, for those who are called
> according to his purpose.*
> **(Romans 8:28)**

As we dwell on the message of the gospel, we begin to see that we are no longer who we once were. At one time, we were enemies of God. We hated Him. We ignored His voice and chose to go our own way. We rebelled against Him. But now He has drawn us unto Himself. When we trust in Christ and receive His gift of salvation, we are reborn. We are a new creation in Christ.

In Christ we are blameless, holy, loved, and forgiven. Our sin is separated from us as far as the east is from the west. We are granted an inheritance in the kingdom of God that cannot be ruined or stolen from us. We are no longer object of God's wrath, but recipients of His mercy. We are no longer His enemies, but His family.

> *I thank him who has given me strength, Christ Jesus our Lord, because he judged me faithful, appointing me to his service, 13 though formerly I was a blasphemer, persecutor, and insolent opponent. But I received mercy because I had acted ignorantly in unbelief, 14 and the grace of our Lord overflowed for me with the faith and love that are in Christ Jesus. (1 Timothy 1:12-*

14)

*Therefore, if anyone is in Christ, he is a new creation. The old has passed away; behold, the new has come. (**2 Corinthians 5:17**)*

*Blessed be the God and Father of our Lord Jesus Christ, who has blessed us in Christ with every spiritual blessing in the heavenly places, 4 even as he chose us in him before the foundation of the world, that we should be holy and blameless before him. In love 5 he predestined us for adoption as sons through Jesus Christ, according to the purpose of his will, 6 to the praise of his glorious grace, with which he has blessed us in the Beloved. 7 In him we have redemption through his blood, the forgiveness of our trespasses, according to the riches of his grace, 8 which he lavished upon us, (**Ephesians 1:3-8a**)*

So does this mean that even though I tend to define myself through the lens of my failures and mistakes that God sees me differently? **Yes!**

Does this mean that though I regularly tell myself that I am unloved and unlovable that Jesus in fact loves me? **Yes!**

Does this mean that even though I like to tell myself that I'm all alone that God is always with me and has adopted me into His family? **Yes!**

Does this mean that even though I make a practice of condemning myself, I am in fact not condemned if I truly believe in Christ Jesus? **Yes!**

These are such wonderful truths that are essential facets of the gospel. We don't remind ourselves of these things often enough, but the Lord wants these truths to be on the forefront of our minds, not stuffed away in some sort of distant mental cabinet. Just imagine how different our lives would be if these were the dominant thoughts in our minds?

Practical suggestions

Practically speaking, you'll need to be very intentional about meditating on the truth of the gospel and I'd like to make a few suggestions that might help you to do so. The first suggestion is something that I briefly referenced earlier in this chapter.

How do you typically start your day? Most of us begin our day with a flurry of activity. We usually stay in bed until the very last second then we jump up and rush through our morning routine with the goal of getting out of the door and to our place of employment before it's time to clock in.

A better solution is to **carve out a few minutes at the start of each day**, before rushing into all of your "must do" activity, to spend time in the Scriptures and in prayer. I'm not talking an hour or even thirty minutes (although if you feel ambitious, that would be a great option). I'm actually just suggesting 5-10 minutes that follows this pattern:

*Prayer focused on thanking the Lord for who He is (**1 minute**)

*Prayer of confession and repentance, recognizing that you're communicating with the person who loves you most (**1 minute**)

*Prayer of thankfulness for how God is working in your life and how He has shown Himself to be faithful to you (**1 minute**)

*Read one chapter of the Bible, working your way through it one book at a time (**5 minutes**)

*Prayer focused on requesting the Lord's help and strength throughout the new day (**2 minutes**)

This pattern of prayer and Scripture meditation is a powerful way to begin your day. Ironically, many Christians don't bother to do so - largely because they consider this to be an intimidating exercise and they're convinced that they don't have time for it. Because their expectation is that prayer and Scripture reading need to be lengthy to be meaningful, they delay doing so which results in them not bothering to do so at all.

But when we begin our morning engaging in a time of focused worship, we're establishing a pattern for our thinking for the rest of our day. If it becomes our regular routine to start each morning dwelling on the truth God has revealed as well as His active presence in our lives, we're engaging in a spiritual exercise that can help us "think on things above" all throughout our day.

Another practical suggestion that might benefit you is the practice of **creating a written reminder that focuses on the eternal truths that you most often tend to forget**. (Writing or typing this list out and putting it in a plastic sleeve or sending it to your smart phone as a document might be very helpful.)

What aspects of the gospel do you find yourself most likely to forget? God's mercy and grace? Your new identity in Christ? The process of transformation the Holy Spirit is bringing you through? The fact that God has made you part of His family? The fact that God is always present with you? The fact that you are a new creation in Christ and no longer the person you used to be? The fact that your value isn't anchored to a shifting worldly standard?

Whatever aspect or application of the gospel you find yourself forgetting is a great candidate for inclusion on this list. Whenever you're tempted to start engaging in negative self-talk that is the fruit of failing to apply the gospel to some aspect of your life, retrieve your list and take a moment to read it. Refresh your mind and challenge your thinking.

Meditating on the truth of the gospel is something that we truly cannot do enough. Feed your mind a stead diet of this truth. Welcome it as a healthy source of nourishment to your soul. Commit it to memory and let it counteract the falsehoods you've spent far too much of your life dwelling on.

JOHN STANGE

Chapter 11.
Step Seven: Repeat the truth of the Gospel to the same person

A few chapters ago, I suggested an intervention that involved a friend. My suggestion was to sit down with your friend, explain your battle with negative self-talk, and ask them to sit through a reading of the list of negative statements that you typically say to yourself (while directing those statements toward them).

Most people who take the time to follow through with this exercise indicate that it had a powerful impact on their tendency to engage in negative self-talk. It tends to become much more difficult for them to treat their self-talk as innocent, passive or harmless once they've seen the way it can impact someone else when it's spoken out loud. They picture their friend's face and they remember the grief they shared after going through this experience together.

In the time since you went through this exercise with your friend, you have had additional time for reflection and meditation. You've been reflecting on the source of your negative self-talk, trying to identify where it came from or what life experiences it might be linked to. You've also had time to meditate on the truth of the gospel and dwell on the subject of who God is and how He lovingly operates in your life.

Having done so, my hope is that you have developed greater understanding of some of your personal blind spots and even more importantly, I hope your application of the truth of the gospel has become more pronounced in both your beliefs and behavior.

Now it's time to invite your friend back for another conversation - a conversation that is meant to prompt your hearts to rejoice. A conversation that gives you an opportunity to proclaim the truth that you have been hesitating to embrace for far too long. Just as it was meaningful to verbalize your negative self-talk, I believe it can be redemptive to verbalize the truth of the gospel to the very same person who was willing to sit and grieve with you during the earlier steps of this process.

The new conversation

Invite your friend to come and speak with you and explain to them that you'd like to have a new conversation based on the truth you've been meditating on since you last met.

Sit down and begin by paraphrasing the story of redemption as presented in Scripture. In your own words, begin by summarizing these key points in the narrative:

> *God's eternal, unchanging, holiness and perfection
>
> *God's decision to speak creation into existence
>
> *God's decision to create mankind in His image
>
> *God's desire to have perfect fellowship with mankind
>
> *Man's rebellion against God and the condition we find ourselves in when He isn't Lord of our life

*God's righteous standard that we could never meet in our own strength

*God's loving and humble intervention in human history through the incarnation of Jesus Christ

*The perfect life, gruesome death and victorious resurrection of Jesus Christ

*Christ's offer to share His victory over sin, Satan and death with all who will come to Him in faith

*The fact that once we believe in Jesus Christ, we become a new creation in Him

*The fact that one day, Jesus will return and will restore His creation to the state He desired for it when He first spoke it into existence

Why do you suppose I think it's valuable to share that information? Am I trying to encourage you to become a theologian? Not necessarily, although there isn't anything wrong with that. What I want you to do at the onset of this conversation is to verbally describe **God's "big-picture" plan** for His creation. It's good to do this because it is a testimony to His goodness, sovereignty, and compassion as well as a reminder of the fact that God is working out a perfect plan and we have a privilege to be part of it.

Once you've verbalized the big-picture plan of God, continue by sharing with your friend **how you fit into God's overall plan**. How He has shown you compassion, reached out to you when you were wandering, drawn you unto Himself, embraced you, called you His child, forgave your sin, clothed you in righteousness and granted you an inheritance in His eternal kingdom.

Tell your friend more about your real identity. At one time, you tried to base your sense of identity around worldly priorities like appearance, power, wealth, education and abilities, but now you see yourself through the lens of being united to Jesus by faith. In Christ, you are free. In Christ, you are forgiven. In Christ, you are blameless. In Christ, you are holy. In Christ you are a new creation.

After testifying to these eternal and edifying truths, revisit the statements you directed toward your friend the last time you met, and restate those sentences through the lens of the gospel.

If you told your friend, *"You look terrible,"* you can now tell them, *"When the Father looks at you, He seeks His Son Jesus Christ. You are holy and blameless in His sight."*

If you told your friend, *"You will always be defined by your mistakes,"* you can now say, *"In Christ, your sins have been removed from you as far as the East is from the West. They are no longer counted against you and the Lord remembers them no more."*

If you told your friend, *"You're poor and you always will be,"* you can say, *"In Christ, you have an eternal inheritance that cannot be corrupted. It is greater than anything in this world. Your life does not consist in the accumulation of worldly things. Your value is found in Christ, not possessions."*

If you told your friend, *"You lack intelligence and should be embarrassed by your stupidity,"* you can now say, *"You have been granted the mind of Christ the moment you trusted in Him. The Holy Spirit is your Counselor and He is granting you wisdom far beyond the most prominent thinking of this age."*

These are just a few examples of what I'm suggesting. There are many more comments you could add to the discussion. The point of this exercise is to communicate the ultimate truth, the truth of the gospel, in such a way as to display it's power over the lies of the false gospels we're all prone to believe.

As you do so, you'll hopefully be encouraging your friend, but you're also giving yourself an opportunity to **visibly observe and audibly hear a proclamation of truth that confronts and contradicts the lies of your negative self-talk**.

Where do you go from here?

As you've been walking through the content of this book and the steps I'm suggesting to help you overcome the power of negative self-talk with the truth of the gospel, you've followed a pattern that includes these seven steps:

1. **You've acknowledged your pain.**

2. **You've examined your beliefs.**

3. **You've identified the negative things you tend to say to yourself.**

4. **You've repeated these negative statements to someone you love and trust.**

5. **You've identified the source of your negative self-talk.**

6. **You've meditated on the**

truth of the Gospel.

7. You've repeated the truth of the gospel to the same person you shared your negative self-talk with.

It is my belief that this is a powerful process to walk through if you're serious about moving beyond the lies you've been led to believe about yourself. I'm convinced that only the truth of the gospel is powerful enough to counteract the deception of the false gospels that we often believe and repeat to ourselves.

After going through this process, I would suggest incorporating many of these suggestions into your daily life and routine. Keep examining your beliefs and holding them up to the light of the gospel. When you find yourself drifting toward the utilization of negative self-talk, ask the Lord to bring to mind the truth of your eternal identity in Christ.

Find creative ways to remind yourself of the truth of the gospel. Surround yourself with people who speak the message of the gospel into your life. Fill your mind with gospel-centered teaching in the form of Scripture study, sermons and good books. Listen to music that prompts you to praise Jesus for His goodness toward you.

Throughout the course of our lives, negative self-talk is something that we all wrestle with to one degree or another. But Jesus Himself secured our victory over the lies we once thought were true and He invites us to continually delight in Him while looking forward to all He has promised to accomplish. He is transforming our minds and teaching us to dwell on things above. As He does so, we're encouraged to continually trust in Him to accomplish this good work in our lives. May everything we believe, think and do be for His glory alone.

--

Can I ask for a favor?

Thank you for taking the time to read these pages. If you enjoyed this book, would you be willing to share your review on Amazon?

Your reviews help others to decide what is worth the time to read. Amazon also makes a point to highlight books that receive ample reviews. If this is a book that you think others would benefit from reading, taking a moment to write a review (even if it's just a couple sentences), goes a long way toward making that happen.

Thank you for your help! I look forward to personally reading your review once it's posted and I hope we have the opportunity to interact more via my Facebook page and my website.

Sincerely,
John Stange

If you enjoy this book, you may also enjoy some of John Stange's other books, including...

Overcoming Anxiety
12 powerful truths from Scripture for defeating worry and fear

Words that Sting
How to handle destructive criticism like Jesus

Building a Christ Centered Marriage
7 Keys for keeping Jesus at the center of your relationship

Everyday Faith (Volume 1)
31 Daily Devotions from the Book of Jude

Too Busy for What Matters Most
6 Priorities of the Christian Life that We Must Make Time for Today

What is Heaven Really Like?
Biblical Answers to the 10 Biggest Questions about Life After Death

Your Identity in Christ
100 Powerful Reminders of Who you Truly are in Jesus

What did Jesus say about Marriage?
What did Christ teach about marriage and how

should I live in response.

Praying what Jesus Prayed for the Church
A devotional look at Christ's prayer in John 17

~

Follow John Stange on Facebook and you'll be notified of his new releases, reduced prices and free book promotions.
https://www.facebook.com/author.john.stange

If you're interested in contacting the author or learning more about his ministry and other books, be sure to visit his website:
JohnStange.com

Bonus Section 1:
Encouraging scriptures
to meditate on

Joshua 1:9

Have I not commanded you? Be strong and courageous. Do not be frightened, and do not be dismayed, for the Lord your God is with you wherever you go."

2 Timothy 1:7

For God gave us a spirit not of fear but of power and love and self-control.

Psalm 121:1-8

A Song of Ascents. I lift up my eyes to the hills. From where does my help come? My help comes from the Lord, who made heaven and earth. He will not let your foot be moved; he who keeps you will not slumber. Behold, he who keeps Israel will neither slumber nor sleep. The Lord is your keeper; the Lord is your shade on your right hand.

Psalm 37:4

Delight yourself in the Lord, and he will give you the desires of your heart.

Proverbs 30:5

Every word of God proves true; he is a shield to those who take refuge in him.

Psalm 28:7

The Lord is my strength and my shield; in him my heart trusts, and I am helped; my heart exults, and with my song I give thanks to him.

Psalm 34:4
I sought the Lord, and he answered me and delivered me from all my fears.

Philippians 4:13
I can do all things through him who strengthens me.

Mark 11:24

Therefore I tell you, whatever you ask in prayer, believe that you have received it, and it will be yours.

1 Thessalonians 5:9-11

For God has not destined us for wrath, but to obtain salvation through our Lord Jesus Christ, who died for us so that whether we are awake or asleep we might live with him. Therefore encourage one another and build one another up, just as you are doing.

Psalm 55:22
Cast your burden on the Lord, and he will sustain you; he will never permit the righteous to be moved.

Romans 15:13
May the God of hope fill you with all joy and peace in believing, so that by the power of the Holy Spirit you may abound in hope.

Psalm 126:5

Those who sow in tears shall reap with shouts of joy!

Hebrews 4:12

For the word of God is living and active, sharper than any two-edged sword, piercing to the division of soul and of spirit, of joints and of marrow, and discerning the thoughts and intentions of the heart.

Jeremiah 29:11-14

For I know the plans I have for you, declares the Lord, plans for welfare and not for evil, to give you a future and a hope. Then you will call upon me and come and pray to me, and I will hear you. You will seek me and find me, when you seek me with all your heart. I will be found by you, declares the Lord, and I will restore your fortunes and gather you from all the nations and all the places where I have driven you, declares the Lord, and I will bring you back to the place from which I sent you into exile.

Hebrews 10:25
Not neglecting to meet together, as is the habit of some, but encouraging one another, and all the more as you see the Day drawing near.

Ephesians 4:29
Let no corrupting talk come out of your mouths, but only such as is good for building up, as fits the occasion, that it may give grace to those who hear.

Romans 15:4
For whatever was written in former days was written for our instruction, that through endurance and through the encouragement of the Scriptures we might have hope.

John 16:33
I have said these things to you, that in me you may have peace. In the world you will have tribulation. But take heart; I have overcome the world."

1 John 2:17

And the world is passing away along with its desires, but whoever does the will of God abides forever.

2 Thessalonians 2:16-17

Now may our Lord Jesus Christ himself, and God our Father, who loved us and gave us eternal comfort and good hope through grace, comfort your hearts and establish them in every good work and word.

Psalm 19:14

Let the words of my mouth and the meditation of my heart be acceptable in your sight, O Lord, my rock and my redeemer.

Romans 15:4-5

For whatever was written in former days was written for our instruction, that through endurance and through the encouragement of the Scriptures we might have hope. May the God of endurance and encouragement grant you to live in such harmony with one another, in accord with Christ Jesus,

John 3:16-17

"For God so loved the world, that he gave his only Son, that whoever believes in him should not perish but have eternal life. For God did not send his Son into the world to condemn the world, but in order that the world might be saved through him.

Hebrews 6:18

So that by two unchangeable things, in which it is impossible for God to lie, we who have fled for refuge might have strong encouragement to hold fast to the hope set before us.

2 Corinthians 4:16-18

So we do not lose heart. Though our outer self is wasting away, our inner self is being renewed day by day. For this light momentary affliction is preparing for us an eternal weight of glory beyond all comparison, as we look not to the things that are seen but to the things that are unseen. For the things that are seen are transient, but the things that are unseen are eternal.

Zephaniah 3:17

The Lord your God is in your midst, a mighty one who will save; he will rejoice over you with gladness; he will quiet you by his love; he will exult over you with loud singing.

1 Timothy 4:12

Let no one despise you for your youth, but set the believers an example in speech, in conduct, in love, in faith, in purity.

John 15:13
Greater love has no one than this, that someone lay down his life for his friends.

Jeremiah 33:3
Call to me and I will answer you, and will tell you great and hidden things that you have not known.

Ephesians 5:1-33
Therefore be imitators of God, as beloved children. And walk in love, as Christ loved us and gave himself up for us, a fragrant offering and sacrifice to God. But sexual immorality and all impurity or covetousness must not even be named among you, as is proper among saints. Let there be no filthiness nor foolish talk nor crude joking, which are out of place, but instead let there be thanksgiving. For you may be sure of this, that everyone who is sexually immoral or impure, or who is covetous (that is, an idolater), has no inheritance in the kingdom of Christ and God.

1 Corinthians 14:31

For you can all prophesy one by one, so that all may learn and all be encouraged,

Ecclesiastes 3:1-3

For everything there is a season, and a time for every matter under heaven: a time to be born, and a time to die; a time to plant, and a time to pluck up what is planted; a time to kill, and a time to heal; a time to break down, and a time to build up;

1 Thessalonians 5:11

Therefore encourage one another and build one another up, just as you are doing.

Ephesians 6:4

Fathers, do not provoke your children to anger, but bring them up in the discipline and instruction of the Lord.

Deuteronomy 6:6-7

And these words that I command you today shall be on your heart. You shall teach them diligently to your children, and shall talk of them when you sit in your house, and when you walk by the way, and when you lie down, and when you rise.

1 Peter 2:3

If indeed you have tasted that the Lord is good.

Galatians 6:2

Bear one another's burdens, and so fulfill the law of Christ.

Acts 4:12

And there is salvation in no one else, for there is no other name under heaven given among men by which we must be saved."

Isaiah 43:18-19

"Remember not the former things, nor consider the things of old. Behold, I am doing a new thing; now it springs forth, do you not perceive it? I will make a way in the wilderness and rivers in the desert.

Philippians 1:6

And I am sure of this, that he who began a good work in you will bring it to completion at the day of Jesus Christ.

Bonus Section 2:
Sample from the book,
"Overcoming Anxiety"
by John Stange

Pray with Thankfulness

Philippians 4:6-7

Do not be anxious about anything, but in everything by prayer and supplication with thanksgiving let your requests be made known to God. And the peace of God, which surpasses all understanding, will guard your hearts and your minds in Christ Jesus.

Anxiety is painful. It is a real struggle for all of us to one degree or another. Some of us are better at hiding our anxiety than others, but we all struggle with it.

The Lord's desire for us is that we trade our anxiety for His peace. He offers to guard our hearts and minds in Christ Jesus so that we won't be consumed by the worries of this world. But how is that trade initiated? How can we trade the paralysis of worry for the blessing of peace?

This Scripture reminds us to come to the Lord in prayer. It may be that you have been going through your life up to this point trying to carry a heavy burden that you were never meant to carry in the first place. Jesus came to bear the burdens that we often try to carry. He invites us to give those burdens over to Him in prayer. He encourages us to let our requests be made known to Him in a spirit of thanksgiving.

Why does He ask us to pray with thankfulness? As I look at this verse, I can't help but wonder if He's asking us to be thankful in the sense that our thankfulness intrinsically expresses confidence that the Lord already has the very things we're praying about worked out. It's like we're thanking Him in advance for what we already know He is going to accomplish. It's an expression that seems to be directly connected to our faith.

And as we pray, the Lord assures us that He will guard our hearts and minds. Anxiety tends to multiply in our hearts and minds like bacteria in a petri dish. Jesus assures us that He will supernaturally guard our hearts to prevent that from happening as we entrust our concerns to Him.

Bonus Section 3:
Sample from the book, "Too Busy for what Matters Most"
by John Stange

Priority 1: Don't Be Too Busy to Invest in Your Health

1. Investing in our spiritual health

> *And so, from the day we heard, we have not ceased to pray for you, asking that you may be filled with the knowledge of his will in all spiritual wisdom and understanding,* **(Colossians 1:9)**

Several years ago, I decided to start teaching my children about saving and investing. I opened up individual accounts for them with an investment foundation where they earn 2% on their money and I encouraged them to save as much as possible. Their saving is paying off. They love when they get their statements in the mail and I'm pretty sure that each of my children could tell you exactly how much interest they earned last year from their investment.

There are even greater benefits that come to our lives through what is being invested on the spiritual level. For years, the Apostle Paul travelled around the Roman Empire, sharing the gospel. He taught, discipled and trained new believers. He encouraged them to do the same for others and as a result, many people in the Empire came to faith in Christ.

Epaphras was one such person Paul had invested in, possibly during his time ministering in the city of Ephesus. Just prior to Paul writing the book of Colossians, Epaphras had come looking for him, even though Paul was in prison at the time, to tell him about the church that had been started in Colosse.

I'm certain that Paul was thrilled when this news of a new church being planted reached his ears. In the midst of his imprisonment, the Lord was bringing him much needed encouragement. And ever since Paul had received the good news of the founding of the church at Colosse, he prayed faithfully for them. He knew that they were young in the faith. He knew that there was much about Jesus that they probably didn't yet understand. He realized that their faith was probably being tested from all angles as they lived and worked in an area that was known for its licentiousness. So he prayed for them daily.

His prayer for them is something that I would encourage you to pray for yourself, your spouse and your children. As a father, I want my children to grow up to love Christ and to have a deep, mature faith in Him. But I know that takes time and that certainly isn't something that would be automatically true of them in their youth. Paul loved this church like a father so he prayed that they would be filled with the knowledge of God's will, wisdom and understanding.

How can that be true of us as well? We're busy people, but investments need to be made in our spiritual health if we're going to grow. Growth isn't as complicated as we often make it. It begins with simple, childlike-faith in the Author of life - Jesus Christ

And they were bringing children to him that he might touch them, and the disciples rebuked them. But when Jesus saw it, he was indignant and said to them, "Let the children come to me; do not hinder them, for to such belongs the kingdom of God. Truly, I say to you, whoever does not receive the kingdom of God like a child shall not enter it." And he took them in his arms and blessed them, laying his hands on them. **(Mark 10:13-16)**

Growth continues through spending intentional time with Him through prayer and looking into His Word. It is strengthened through relationships with other believers and it's deepened by living your faith in Christ out and being strengthened by Him to actively serve others.

For Christ's glory and with His power, make investments in your spiritual health.

2. Investing in our emotional health

*so as to walk in a manner worthy
of the Lord, fully pleasing to him,
bearing fruit in every good work
and increasing in the knowledge
of God.* **(Colossians 1:10)**

Walking is something that I truly enjoy doing. When I was growing up, I felt like I knew every street and short-cut in my town. I walked everywhere. I delivered newspapers, visited friends and then sometimes I took long walks when I didn't know what else to do with my time. I walked in the rain and the snow. It didn't matter to me. I just enjoyed it. I once told a friend that, using side streets and shortcuts, I could make it from his house to my house in a different section of town before a particular song was finished playing on the radio. He didn't believe me, but I proved it to him by calling him from my house before the song was finished playing.

Scripture uses the concept of "walking" to illustrate something of a deeper spiritual significance. It's a term that refers to how we live and conduct ourselves. Specifically, we're being told here that we are to walk or live in a manner that:

1. Is worthy of the Lord,
2. Is fully pleasing to Him,
3. Bears fruit in every good work,
4. Is increasing in the knowledge of God.

There are two ways to approach a verse like that, and I have attempted both approaches. One approach is helpful and effective. The other approach will drive you crazy. Many people select the crazy approach.

The crazy or "drive-you-crazy" approach is to try to do this without help. Try to live your life worthy of the Lord. Try to please Him in all things. Try to do good works. Try to increase in your knowledge of Him and do this all without seeking help and with total reliance on your own strength and perceived abilities. I'm telling you, that approach will drive you nuts and it isn't the way of new life in Christ - even though it may look very spiritual to others from the outside.

The effective approach is where you come to a

place of humility where you realize that you can't do any of this without Christ. Without the coaching, empowerment and wisdom of the Holy Spirit, you will become self-righteous and very harsh and judgmental as you seek to live this out. You will develop very unhealthy spiritual traits and emotional responses. But with the Holy Spirit's help, based on the eternal truth of the Gospel of Christ, you can walk in the manner "worthy of the Lord."

> *But he said to me, "My grace is sufficient for you, for my power is made perfect in weakness." Therefore I will boast all the more gladly of my weaknesses, so that the power of Christ may rest upon me.* (**2 Corinthians 12:9**)

> *But you will receive power when the Holy Spirit has come upon you, and you will be my witnesses in Jerusalem and in all Judea and Samaria, and to the end of the earth.* (**Acts 1:8**)

> *If any of you lacks wisdom, let*

*him ask God, who gives generously to all without reproach, and it will be given him. (**James 1:5**)*

The Gospel tells us that Jesus came to rescue sinners who could never save themselves. Our emotional health is directly affected by our perspective on this message of truth. If you view the Gospel as something in the category of "infancy" or "lunacy", your emotional health will suffer. If you view it through the lens of the daily nourishment that your heart has the privilege of delighting in, you will notice a healthy impact on your emotional health.

You will experience joy in knowing that, in Christ, you are pleasing to your Heavenly Father. You will live as one who grasps the reality of what it means to be forgiven, cleansed, satisfied, adopted and accepted into God's family. When those aspects of the Gospel sink into your heart and mind, your emotional health is impacted supernaturally.

3. Investing in our physical health

May you be strengthened with all power, according to his glorious might, for all endurance and patience with joy, 12 giving thanks to the Father, who has qualified you to share in the inheritance of the saints in light. 13 He has delivered us from the domain of darkness and transferred us to the kingdom of his beloved Son, 14 in whom we have redemption, the forgiveness of sins. **(Colossians 1:11-14)**

I probably shouldn't admit this, because you'll probably start holding me accountable for it, but generally speaking, I have been attempting to incorporate some better dietary habits into my weekly food rotation. I make generous exceptions for church dinners, holidays and other special events, but other than that, I have been cutting most sugar and flour out of my diet. I tend to stress eat, so limiting the flour and sugar I'm eating has also eliminated most of the unhealthy things that I would be tempted to snack on. I very well may drift off the wagon at some point, but for now, I'm trying to invest in my physical health. I bring this up because there are spiritual, emotional and physical implications to what Paul expresses in this passage.

Paul prayed for this young church that they would be strengthened with all power, giving thanks to God the Father who has delivered us from the kingdom of darkness to the kingdom of His Son, Jesus Christ. What kind of physical implications could there be in our lives from something that seems to be primarily speaking of spiritual realities?

Most evenings, I take about 10-15 minutes to discuss a portion of Scripture with my kids. Recently, we were looking at the book of 1 John and we came across these verses:

> *whoever says he abides in him ought to walk in the same way in which he walked.* (*1 John 2:6*)

> *Whoever loves his brother abides in the light, and in him there is no cause for stumbling. 11 But whoever hates his brother is in*

the darkness and walks in the darkness, and does not know where he is going, because the darkness has blinded his eyes. (1 John 2:10-11)

We discussed that these verses encourage us to live our lives in this world in a way that truly mirrors Jesus. And further, we're to remember that once we are in Him, we are in the light. We are no longer in the darkness and therefore we don't need to live like we're ruled by the darkness of sin.

That same truth is expressed in a different, but related way in Colossians 1:13. We're told here that we were once living as members of Satan's domain of darkness. When you're part of a domain, that means you're being dominated by something. We were dominated and under the control of evil. The intentions of our heart, the thoughts of our minds and the actions of our bodies proved that to be true. But the moment we receive Christ, trusting that He is God, receiving His forgiveness, we are transferred to the domain of a new kingdom. We are delivered from darkness and qualified through

Jesus to live in His kingdom of light - forever.

And when this deliverance takes place for you, you won't be at peace with using your body as an instrument for sin. You won't be at peace with your body being dominated by darkness because you have tasted the flavor of your new life in Christ and life in His kingdom surpasses all else.

> *"Oh, taste and see that the Lord is good! Blessed is the man who takes refuge in him!"* **(Psalm 34:8)**

You're busy and I'm busy and the busier we are, the faster our time seems to escape us. But let's not be too busy for what really matters. Let's not be too busy to invest in our spiritual, emotional and physical health. Let's not be too busy to recognize the investment that the Lord has made, is making and wants to make. Allow Him to. Invite Him to. Taste and see that He is good.

Personal Reflection and Notes

Personal Reflection and Notes

Personal Reflection and Notes

Personal Reflection and Notes

Personal Reflection and Notes

Personal Reflection and Notes

Personal Reflection and Notes

Personal Reflection and Notes

Printed in Great Britain
by Amazon

64774952R00098